BIKE PORN

MOUNTAIN BIKES

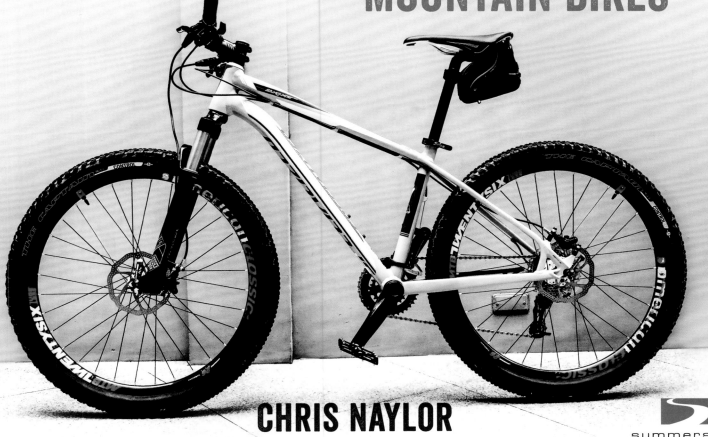

CHRIS NAYLOR

summersdale

BIKE PORN: MOUNTAIN BIKES

Picture research by Sam Dugon

Summersdale Publishers Ltd
46 West Street
Chichester
West Sussex
PO19 1RP
UK

www.summersdale.com

Printed and bound in China

ISBN: 978-1-84953-743-8

Substantial discounts on bulk quantities of Summersdale books are available to corporations, professional associations and other organisations. For details contact Nicky Douglas by telephone: +44 (0) 1243 756902, fax: +44 (0) 1243 786300 or email: nicky@summersdale.com.

INTRODUCTION

THE BEAUTY OF A BICYCLE IS AS SYMBOLIC AS IT IS PHYSICAL. THE UNTRAINED EYE CAN LOOK AT A PERFECTLY MADE BIKE AND SEE ELEGANCE, SLEEK DESIGN AND UNDENIABLE CRAFTSMANSHIP. TO THE BIKE LOVER, HOWEVER, THE PICTURE IS MUCH RICHER THAN THAT: IN THE CURVE OF A HANDLEBAR IS CONTROL AND STRENGTH, THE SHINING WEAVE OF SPOKES CONJURES POWER AND ADRENALINE, SMOOTH LINES OF THE FRAME CONTAIN AS MUCH HEART AS THE RIDER ATOP IT. THIS BOOK CELEBRATES THE MOUNTAIN BIKES THAT DON'T JUST MAKE YOU CATCH YOUR BREATH WHEN RIDING THEM, BUT ON SIGHT AS WELL. FROM THE SMALLEST SCREW TO THE MOST TECHNOLOGICALLY CUTTING-EDGE FRAME, EVERY INCH OF THESE BIKES SPEAKS TO THE PASSION AND SKILL OF THOSE WHO MAKE AND RIDE THEM.

'TO BE PRECISE AND RECKLESS: THAT IS THE CONSUMMATION DEVOUTLY TO BE WISHED.'

JAMES DICKEY

'SPEED PROVIDES THE
ONE GENUINELY MODERN
PLEASURE.'

ALDOUS HUXLEY

'A BAD DAY ON THE MOUNTAIN BIKE ALWAYS BEATS A GOOD DAY IN THE OFFICE.'

MIKE BRCIC

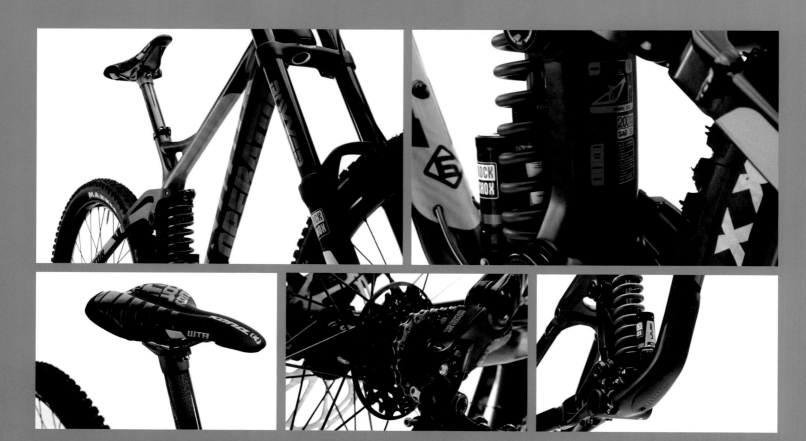

'THE SECRET TO MOUNTAIN BIKING IS PRETTY SIMPLE – THE SLOWER YOU GO THE MORE LIKELY IT IS YOU'LL CRASH.'

JULI FURTADO

'THE BICYCLE IS A CURIOUS INVENTION. ITS PASSENGER IS ITS ENGINE.'

JOHN HOWARD

'IT IS EASY TO BE A HOLY MAN ON A MOUNTAIN BIKE.'

MARK W. WATSON

'IT IS BY RIDING A BICYCLE THAT YOU LEARN THE CONTOURS OF A COUNTRY BEST, SINCE YOU HAVE TO SWEAT UP THE HILLS AND COAST DOWN THEM.'

ERNEST HEMINGWAY

'THERE IS NOTHING, ABSOLUTELY NOTHING, QUITE SO WORTHWHILE AS SIMPLY MESSING ABOUT ON BICYCLES.'

TOM KUNICH

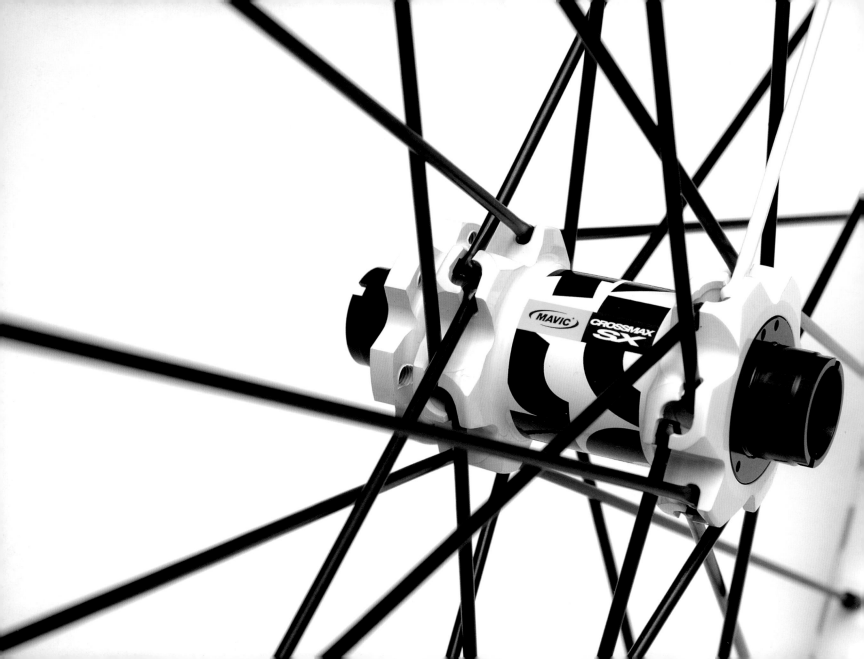

'CYCLE TRACKS WILL ABOUND IN UTOPIA.'

H. G. WELLS

'THERE'S NO SUCH THING AS BAD WEATHER, JUST SOFT PEOPLE.'

BILL BOWERMAN

'MOUNTAIN BIKING CAN'T BE SQUARE AND CLEAN-CUT 'CAUSE IT'S NOT A SQUARE SPORT. IT'S GOTTA STAY TRIBAL.'

MISSY GIOVE

'LIFE'S TOO SHORT NOT TO GO BIG — YA GOTTA GO BIG.'

JOSH BENDER

'MOUNTAIN BIKING OFFERS RECREATION, FREEDOM, TRANSPORTATION, SPORT AND THE OPPORTUNITY TO GET FAR AWAY FROM IT ALL.'

CHARLIE KELLY

'WHEN YOU'RE TURNING THE CRANKSET, YOU'RE RIDING THE BIKE. WHEN YOU'RE COASTING, YOU'RE JUST ALONG FOR THE RIDE.'

NED OVEREND

'IF CONSTELLATIONS
HAD BEEN NAMED IN THE
TWENTIETH CENTURY,
I SUPPOSE WE WOULD
SEE BICYCLES.'

CARL SAGAN

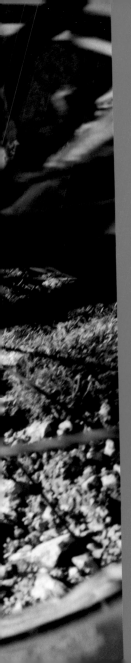

'YOU'RE MOVING THROUGH
A WONDERFUL NATURAL
ENVIRONMENT AND WORKING
ON BALANCE, TIMING, DEPTH
PERCEPTION, JUDGEMENT... IT
FORMS KIND OF A BALLET.'

CHARLIE CUNNINGHAM

'GREAT DESIGN IS MAKING SOMETHING MEMORABLE AND MEANINGFUL.'

DIETER RAMS

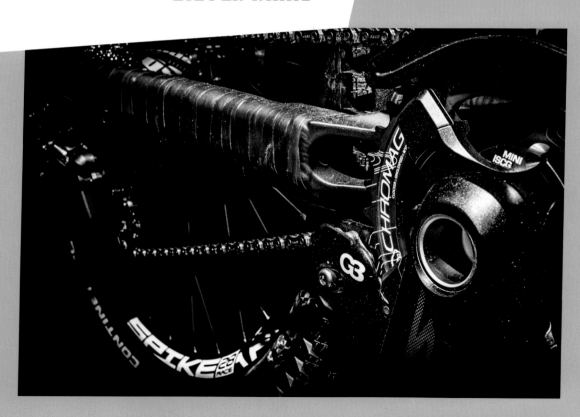

'THE SPIRIT OF MOUNTAIN
BIKING IS COOL.'

SUSAN DEMATTEI

'GOOD BICYCLES TURN EFFORT INTO EMOTION. THEY PROVIDE THE MEANS TO REACH, AND SOMETIMES EXCEED, YOUR POTENTIAL.'

JIM LANGLEY

'SIMPLICITY IS THE ULTIMATE SOPHISTICATION.'

LEONARDO DA VINCI

'GET A BICYCLE. YOU WILL CERTAINLY NOT REGRET IT, IF YOU LIVE.'

MARK TWAIN

'THE DIFFERENCE BETWEEN SOMETHING GOOD AND SOMETHING GREAT IS ATTENTION TO DETAIL.'

CHARLES R. SWINDOLL

'THERE IS NO IMPOSSIBILITY TO HIM WHO STANDS PREPARED TO CONQUER EVERY HAZARD.'

SARAH J. HALE

'GREAT THINGS ARE DONE WHEN MEN AND MOUNTAINS MEET.'

WILLIAM BLAKE

'YOU WANT TO RIDE LIKE
SILK GLIDING ON SOFT AIR.'

HANK BARLOW

'LIFE BEGINS AT THE END OF YOUR COMFORT ZONE.'

NEALE DONALD WALSCH

'**A BICYCLE RIDE AROUND THE WORLD BEGINS WITH A SINGLE PEDAL STROKE.**'

SCOTT STOLL

'A MOUNTAIN BIKE IS
LIKE YOUR BUDDY.'

SEAN COFFEY

'I DON'T HAVE A BUCKET
LIST, BUT MY BIKEIT LIST
IS A MILE LONG.'

ANONYMOUS

'I DON'T RIDE FOR THE MONEY SO MUCH, OR FOR THE FAME. I RIDE FOR MY HEART. I'M A SOUL RIDER.'

STEVE COOK

'POWER AND SPEED BE
HANDS AND FEET.'

RALPH WALDO EMERSON

'IF YOU HAVE DONE YOUR HOMEWORK RIGHT, YOU REALLY DO UNDERSTAND, AT A REASONABLE LEVEL, WHAT'S HAPPENING AND WHY, TO A BIKE OR WHEEL.'

KEITH BONTRAGER

'CHASING ANGELS OR FLEEING DEMONS, GO TO THE MOUNTAINS.'

JEFFREY RASLEY

'WE ARE WHAT WE REPEATEDLY DO. EXCELLENCE, THEREFORE, IS NOT AN ACT, BUT A HABIT.'

ARISTOTLE

'I KNOW MYSELF THROUGH MOUNTAIN BIKING. THAT'S HOW I CENTRE MYSELF IF THINGS ARE OUT OF WHACK PERSONALLY.'

MYLES ROCKWELL

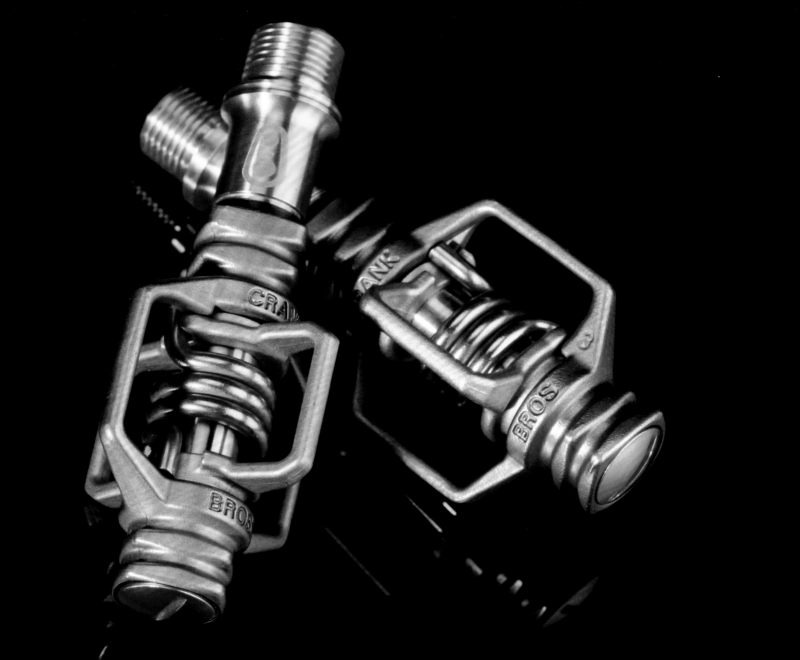

'EVENTUALLY EVERYTHING CONNECTS – PEOPLE, IDEAS, OBJECTS. THE QUALITY OF THE CONNECTIONS IS THE KEY TO QUALITY.'

CHARLES EAMES

'FREEDOM LIES IN BEING BOLD.'

ROBERT FROST

'SPACE IS THE BREATH OF ART.'

FRANK LLOYD WRIGHT

'YOU NEED TO KNOW WHY YOU FALL. IT'S HOW YOU LEARN. IF YOU CRASH AND YOU DON'T KNOW WHY, THAT'S THE TIME TO SLOW AND RELAX AWHILE.'

HANS REY

'BICYCLES HAVE NO WALLS.'

PAUL CORNISH

'LIFE IS A
BEAUTIFUL RIDE.'

ANONYMOUS

'WHOEVER INVENTED THE BICYCLE DESERVES THE THANKS OF HUMANITY.'

CHARLES BERESFORD

'IN ORDER TO SUCCEED, WE MUST FIRST BELIEVE THAT WE CAN.'

NIKOS KAZANTZAKIS

'I LIKE EXTREME, INTENSE SITUATIONS. THE MORE EXTREME, THE BETTER.'

MISSY GIOVE

'I RELAX BY TAKING
MY BICYCLE APART
AND PUTTING IT BACK
TOGETHER AGAIN.'

MICHELLE PFEIFFER

'MOUNTAIN BIKING IS LIKE A DRUG FOR ME. I DO IT BECAUSE I ENJOY IT.'

RUDY DE BIE

'DESIGN IS NOT JUST WHAT IT LOOKS LIKE AND FEELS LIKE. DESIGN IS HOW IT WORKS.'

STEVE JOBS

'IT'S FREEING, THE SENSE OF DETACHED AWARENESS FOUND ONLY ON THE BEST MOUNTAIN-BIKE RIDES. I'M NO LONGER ME. I'M A ROLLING BALL OF INTENT.'

DON CUERDON

'ANYTHING THAT GETS YOUR BLOOD RACING IS PROBABLY WORTH DOING.'

HUNTER S. THOMPSON

'IF IN DOUBT, PEDAL IT OUT.'

ANONYMOUS

'ONCE IT WAS DEMONSTRATED THAT ALUMINIUM AND CARBON WORKED IN MOUNTAIN BIKES, IT JUST TURNED INTO THE WILD, WILD WEST.'

KEITH BONTRAGER

'DESIGN IS NOT FOR
PHILOSOPHY; IT'S
FOR LIFE.'

ISSEY MIYAKE

'FEAR IS ONLY AS DEEP AS THE MIND ALLOWS.'

JAPANESE PROVERB

'ONE OF THE MOST IMPORTANT DAYS OF MY LIFE WAS WHEN I LEARNED TO RIDE A BICYCLE.'

MICHAEL PALIN

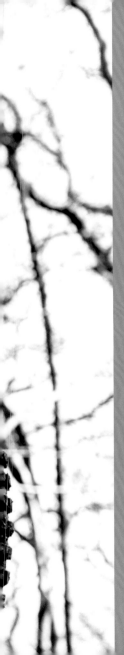

'THE BEST RIDES ARE THE ONES WHERE YOU BITE OFF MUCH MORE THAN YOU CAN CHEW, AND LIVE THROUGH IT.'

DOUG BRADBURY

'THERE IS A HIPPOPOTAMUS IN ME THAT WANTS TO WALLOW IN THE MUD.'

CARL SANDBURG

'EVERYTHING HAS BEAUTY,
BUT NOT EVERYONE SEES IT.'

CONFUCIUS

'BICYCLING IS A BIG PART OF THE FUTURE. IT HAS TO BE.'

BILL NYE

'NEVER USE YOUR FACE
AS A BRAKE PAD.'

JAKE WATSON

'THE BICYCLE IS THE NOBLEST INVENTION OF MANKIND.'

WILLIAM SAROYAN

'MAY YOUR TRAILS BE
CROOKED, WINDING,
LONESOME, DANGEROUS,
LEADING TO THE MOST
AMAZING VIEW.'

EDWARD ABBEY

PHOTO CREDITS

IF YOU'RE INTERESTED IN FINDING OUT MORE ABOUT OUR BOOKS,
FIND US ON FACEBOOK AT *SUMMERSDALE PUBLISHERS*
AND FOLLOW US ON TWITTER AT *@SUMMERSDALE*.

WWW.SUMMERSDALE.COM